EXPEDITION TO THE ARCTIC

Natalie Hyde

CRABTREE
Publishing Company
www.crabtreebooks.com

Crabtree Publishing Company
www.crabtreebooks.com

Author: Natalie Hyde
**Publishing plan research
   and development:** Reagan Miller
Editors: Sonya Newland, Kathy Middleton
Proofreader: Adrianna Morganelli
Photo researchers: Sonya Newland,
   Rachel Minay
Original design: Tim Mayer (Mayer Media)
Book design: Kim Williams (320 Media)
Cover design: Ken Wright
**Production coordinator and
   prepress tecnician:** Ken Wright
Print coordinator: Margaret Amy Salter

Produced for Crabtree Publishing
Company by White-Thomson Publishing

Photographs:
Alamy: Pictorial Press Ltd: p. 24; Corbis:
Tarker: pp. 1, 37; The Print Collector: p. 10;
National Geographic Society: pp. 12–13; Derek
Bayes -Art/Lebrecht Music & Arts: pp. 14–15;
Stapleton Collection: pp. 27, 32–33; Hinrich
Baesemann/dpa: pp. 40–41; Getty Images:
pp. 4–5, 30–31; Time & Life Pictures: pp. 8–9;
De Agostini Picture Library: p. 14; Leemage:
p. 29; Library of Congress: pp. 16–17, 25, 34,
36; New York World-Telegram and the Sun
Newspaper Photograph Collection: p. 26;
Shutterstock: Alex Staroseltsev: back cover;
Vladimir Melnik: pp. 6–7; Antonio Abrignani:
p. 11; Armin Rose: p. 23; Sharon Day: pp. 3,
30; Max Lindenthaler: pp. 34–35; Gentoo
Multimedia Limited: pp. 42–43; outdoorsman:
p. 44(t). Topfoto: Topham Picturepoint: pp.
18–19; The Granger Collection: pp. 20–21, 38;
Wikimedia: 22–23; NARA: 28. SuperStock:
Wolfgang Kaehler: p. 44(b); © National
Maritime Museum, London/The Image
Works: front cover

Library and Archives Canada Cataloguing in Publication

Hyde, Natalie, 1963-, author
      Expedition to the Arctic / Natalie Hyde.

(Crabtree chrome)
Includes index.
Issued in print and electronic formats.
ISBN 978-0-7787-1169-8 (bound).--ISBN 978-0-7787-1177-3 (pbk.).--
ISBN 978-1-4271-8930-1 (pdf).--ISBN 978-1-4271-8922-6 (html)

      1. Arctic regions--Discovery and exploration--Juvenile
literature. 2. Northwest Passage--Discovery and exploration--
Juvenile literature. 3. North Pole--Discovery and exploration--
Juvenile literature. I. Title. II. Series: Crabtree chrome

G639.4.H93 2014   j917.19'04   C2013-907567-4
                                             C2013-907568-2

Library of Congress Cataloging-in-Publication Data

Hyde, Natalie, 1963-
   Expedition to the Arctic / Natalie Hyde.
      pages cm. -- (Crabtree chrome)
   Includes index.
   ISBN 978-0-7787-1169-8 (reinforced library binding) -- ISBN
   978-0-7787-1177-3 (pbk.) -- ISBN 978-1-4271-8930-1 (electronic
   pdf) -- ISBN 978-1-4271-8922-6 (electronic html)
   1. Arctic regions--Discovery and exploration--Juvenile
literature. 2. Explorers--Arctic regions--Biography--Juvenile
literature. I. Title.

   G614.H93 2014
   910.911'3--dc23

                                        2013043394

Crabtree Publishing Company

www.crabtreebooks.com   1-800-387-7650

Printed in Canada/012014/BF20131120

Published in Canada
Crabtree Publishing
616 Welland Ave.
St. Catharines, ON
L2M 5V6

Published in the United States
Crabtree Publishing
PMB 59051
350 Fifth Avenue, 59th Floor
New York, New York 10118

Published in the United Kingdom
Crabtree Publishing
Maritime House
Basin Road North, Hove
BN41 1WR

Published in Australia
Crabtree Publishing
3 Charles Street
Coburg North
VIC 3058

Contents

USA 22

NORTH POLE

Vilhjalmur Stefansson

Frozen World

Trapped!

September 1846. The crews of the ships *Terror* and *Erebus* were uneasy. The ice had trapped them off King William Island in the Northwest Territories, Canada. The huge blocks of ice could crush their hulls and sink the boats. The ships and their crew were trapped in the Arctic.

▲ *A ship that has ice pressing on both sides is called "nipped." Many ships, like the* Erebus *and the* Terror, *were crushed and disappeared forever.*

Never Seen Again

British captain Sir John Franklin knew they would have to winter on the ship. They had to ration their food so it would last. The howling wind and cracking ice made it hard to sleep. They hoped the ice would break up in the spring. It never did. Over a decade later, a search party found only a note saying the ships had been abandoned and Captain Franklin was dead.

Over the years, many ships got trapped in the Arctic ice. Some carried Europeans searching for a quick trade route to Asia. Others were **expeditions** to find out more about the Inuit people, or adventurers trying to reach the North Pole.

expeditions: journeys taken for a special purpose

Always Winter

The Arctic is the area that lies in the very north of our planet. The land there is covered with snow and ice for many months of the year. The Arctic Ocean is frozen solid most of the time. For six months of the year it is almost always light, even at night. For six months it is almost always dark, even during the day.

0   1000 miles

0   1000 kilometers

Sea Routes

RUSSIA

Arctic Ocean

GREENLAND

Arctic Circle

Baffin Bay

ALASKA

Hudson Bay

CANADA

N W E S

◀ *This map shows the Arctic region and the sea routes through it.*

The Top of the World

Only a few animals and **indigenous** people make
their homes in this freezing land. Few plants grow
in the Arctic. None at all grow at the North Pole—
the most northern point on Earth. The climate is
too harsh for many living things to survive there.

▼ *Only a few animals, including polar bears,*
can survive in the freezing far north of our world.

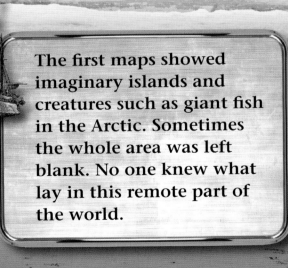

The first maps showed
imaginary islands and
creatures such as giant fish
in the Arctic. Sometimes
the whole area was left
blank. No one knew what
lay in this remote part of
the world.

indigenous: being born in or coming from a particular place

Land of the Midnight Sun

Indigenous peoples, such as the Inuit, have lived in the Arctic for nearly a thousand years. The first white person who may have explored the Arctic was a Greek explorer called Pytheas in about 325 BCE. In his writings, he described a land at the edge of a frozen sea. He was also the first person to mention the Midnight Sun —the Sun that never sets.

Viking Expeditions

The Vikings were very skilled sailors. In their slender ships, they sailed north from Scandinavia to settle in Iceland and Greenland. They also pushed farther north in order to find new trade routes. Their stories, called sagas, describe strange lands that may have been islands in the Arctic.

> "[It is] such a wretched place to live in on account of the cold, that the regions on beyond are regarded as **uninhabitable.**"
>
> Strabo, a Greek geographer, on the Arctic

◀ *A Viking known as Erik the Red established the first settlement in Greenland in around 985 CE.*

uninhabitable: not fit to live in

9

Trade Routes

Europeans began to explore the Arctic **in earnest** to find a new trade route in the 1500s. They wanted to trade goods with Asia. If they sailed west, they were blocked by the continents of North and South America. They hoped that they could find a quicker route across the top of North America, which became known as the Northwest Passage.

▲ *One of the earliest expeditions to find the Northwest Passage was made by Englishman Martin Frobisher in the 1570s. Here, he fights off an attack by the native Arctic people.*

The Northwest Passage

Some explorers were also trying to sail northeast along the coast of Russia. But the Russian government closed the sea route. They were afraid that other countries would use it as a way to invade their country. That left the Northwest Passage as the only way to Asia.

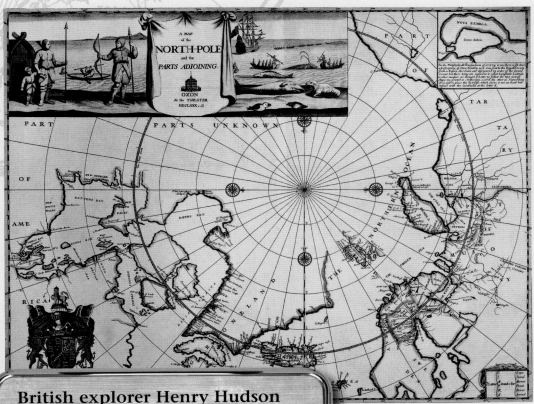

British explorer Henry Hudson discovered Hudson Bay and the Hudson River during his travels in the early 1600s. On his last voyage, his crew turned against him and set him and a few other men adrift in a boat in the Arctic. They were never seen again.

▲ *This map of the Arctic regions was published in 1680. The whole area around the North Pole is marked "Parts Unknown."*

in earnest: make a serious attempt

Franklin's Expedition

Planning the Expedition

Many expeditions were sent to the Arctic to find the Northwest Passage. The expedition of the *Terror* and *Erebus* is one of the most famous. It was led by the British explorer Sir John Franklin. He planned for his trip carefully, packing enough food and supplies to last him and his crew three years.

Franklin Vanishes

A few months after they set out in 1845, the men and ships **vanished**. Several expeditions were sent to try to find them after 1848. The graves of three crew members were found on Beechey Island in the Arctic. Some unburied skeletons were found on nearby King William Island. But Captain Franklin wasn't among them.

> "I do not expect my dear husband to be amongst the survivors—if you should meet with his corpse ... I beg you to bring me his locks of hair."

A letter from Franklin's wife, Lady Jane Franklin, to one of the explorers searching for her husband

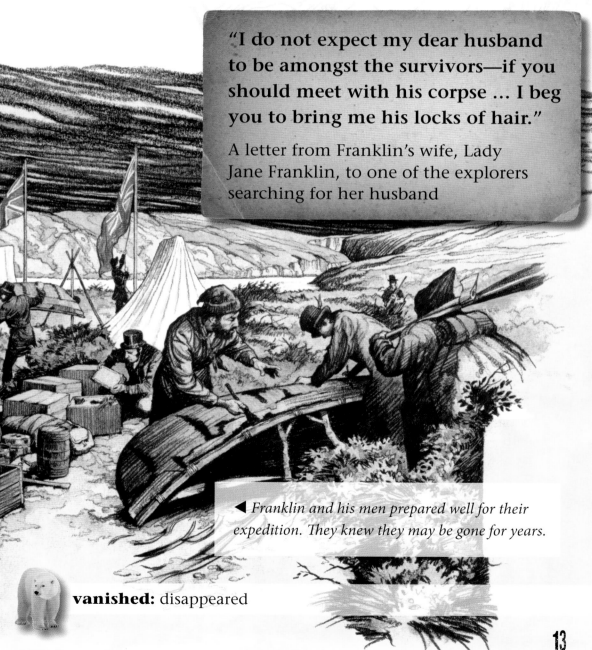

◄ *Franklin and his men prepared well for their expedition. They knew they may be gone for years.*

vanished: disappeared

The Mystery Solved?

For 150 years, people tried to find out what had happened to Franklin's ships and crew. In 1859, a note was found telling of the death of Captain Franklin early in the expedition. It also told of the crew's plan to walk over 1,000 miles (1,600 kilometers) to Back River. They never arrived.

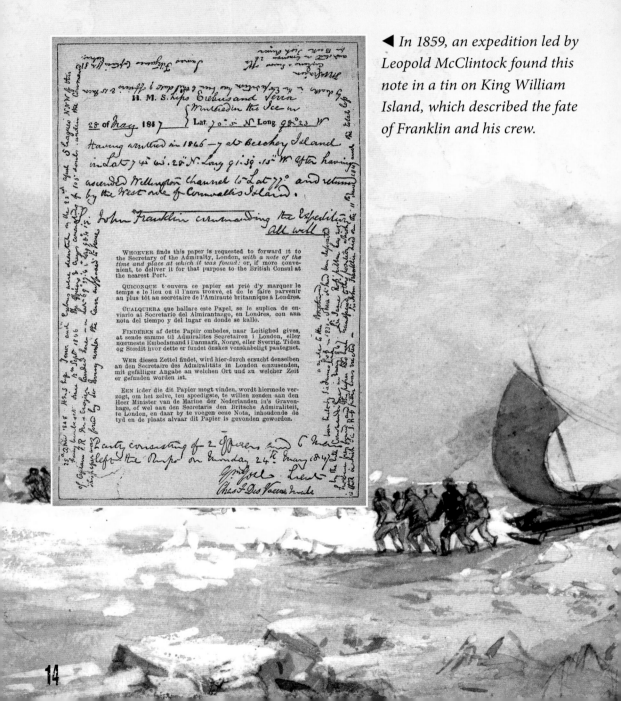

◄ *In 1859, an expedition led by Leopold McClintock found this note in a tin on King William Island, which described the fate of Franklin and his crew.*

Copying the Inuit

Many people believe that if the men had learned skills from the native Inuit people, they would have survived. The Inuit moved around a lot in search of food. They hunted whales and caribou, and traveled in seal-skin boats. They shared their goods with each other in order to survive. Later expeditions **adopted** Inuit ways. This helped them live through long, hard winters when their ships were trapped in ice.

▼ *This picture shows an expedition in search of Franklin in 1853. The searchers have adapted their sleds with sails—a technique they learned from the Inuit.*

The Inuit knew that to survive the cold, a person should wear clothes made of caribou hide and sealskin boots. The European explorers were poorly dressed for the freezing temperatures of the Arctic.

adopted: used as their own

The *Polaris* Expedition

The Race to the North Pole

Some Arctic explorers weren't interested in finding the Northwest Passage. They wanted to get to the North Pole. American Charles Hall was the captain of a ship called the *Polaris*. He wanted to be the first person to reach the Pole. In June 1871, Hall set out from New York on his record-breaking attempt.

Trouble on Board

The *Polaris* sailed to Greenland. Captain Hall dropped anchor for the winter, but there was trouble on board. Some of the men resented Hall's leadership, and the crew split into competing groups. The ship's boiler was **sabotaged** and many of the crew threatened to quit.

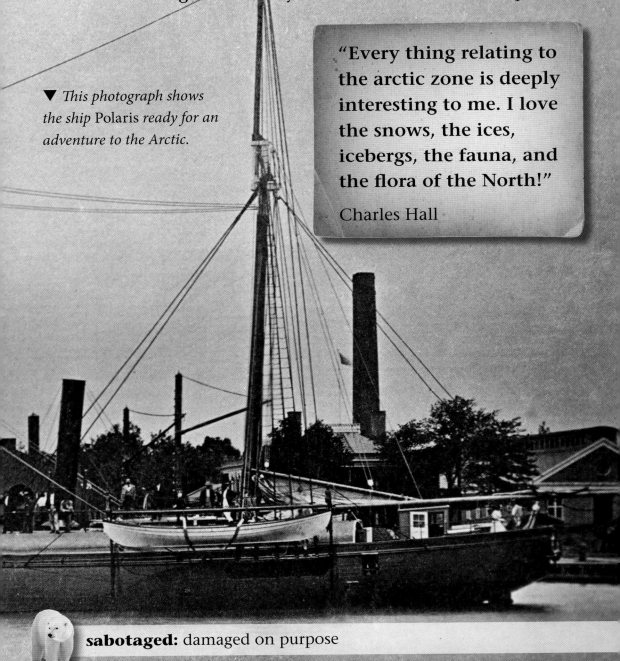

▼ *This photograph shows the ship* Polaris *ready for an adventure to the Arctic.*

"Every thing relating to the arctic zone is deeply interesting to me. I love the snows, the ices, icebergs, the fauna, and the flora of the North!"

Charles Hall

sabotaged: damaged on purpose

Hall's Last Adventure

In Thank God Harbor, Greenland, Hall decided to scout the area. He and three men took two sleds (wooden vehicles on runners that can slide across snow and ice) pulled by dogs. They wanted to go as far north as possible. After traveling some distance, the men turned back. When Hall returned to the ship he grabbed a cup of coffee. It was his last.

▼ *Hall exploring the Arctic using sleds pulled by husky dogs. Here he has an Inuit guide.*

Death by Poison

Within hours, Hall fell sick. He accused the doctor on board of poisoning him. Two weeks later he died. He was buried in a shallow grave in Greenland. The crew did not plan to carry on the expedition. They thought they would return home in the spring. But first they had to survive the winter.

Captain Hall believed someone had poisoned his coffee with **arsenic**. Headaches and stomach cramps lead to coma and eventually death. It was a painful way to die.

arsenic: a gray, poisonous metal

Saving the Ship

The ice pressed hard against the *Polaris*—so hard that the ship almost fell on its side. The men worked to fix the leaks in the **hull**, otherwise the ship would sink. The order was given to "throw everything on the ice!"

▶ *In their panic, the men threw things off the ship without looking where it was going. Much of the cargo was lost.*

Abandoned on the Ice

The men tossed supplies out onto the ice. Suddenly, the ice shifted and the ship broke free. Nineteen people were stranded on a big block of ice. They tried to signal the ship with a black cloth, but the *Polaris* never came back for them.

"The ice broke up again. Our boat and everything we have left are going. We are afloat on a very small piece, with very little provisions left. It is blowing a gale and threatens to be a very severe night."

John Herron, one of the abandoned crew members

hull: the bottom and sides of a ship

Surviving on the Ice

The stranded men and women used the supplies from the ship to survive. The Inuit in their group taught them to build igloos on the **ice floe**. The Inuit also helped them hunt for seals. They used seal blubber for heat and cooking oil.

▼ *This picture is from a book that expedition leader Charles Hall wrote in 1865. It shows an Inuit village on Baffin Island.*

Rescue at Last

After months of drifting along in the Arctic, the ice began to break up. Waves started crashing over the ice, sweeping away the supplies. The survivors couldn't last much longer. Then they saw a steamship, the *Tigress*. After six months, all 19 people were rescued.

▼ *The stranded crew faced a new danger as the ice began to break up and the ocean waves swept over their ice floe.*

"Glorious sight when fog broke; a steamer close to us. She sees us and bears down on us. We are saved, thank God!"

John Herron

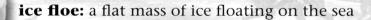

ice floe: a flat mass of ice floating on the sea

The North Pole Challenge

News spread of Captain Hall's failure to reach the North Pole. Other people thought they would take up the challenge. Two Norwegian explorers tried to ski from their ship, which was stuck in ice, but they failed. A Swedish engineer tried to reach the Pole in a **hydrogen** balloon. It crashed and he died.

▲ *Swedish engineer Salomon Andrée and two others set off for the North Pole in a balloon in 1897. All three men died when the balloon crashed.*

Cook's Victory

A U.S. explorer named Frederick Cook set off from Greenland in February 1908. He took two Inuit men with him. No one heard from him for a long time. A year later, he returned. He claimed that he had reached the North Pole in April 1908.

▼ *Cook claimed that this photo was taken near the North Pole. It shows two members of his expedition, with the American flag stuck in an igloo.*

Cook left the records of his trip in Greenland because he couldn't carry them back to the United States. They were never found. Many people doubted that he had really reached the North Pole.

hydrogen: a gas that is lighter than air

Peary's Expedition

Robert Peary was an American explorer. He set off for the
North Pole in April 1909, one month before Cook came back.
Like many other people, Peary was sure that Cook was dead.
Peary took with him 50 men, many sleds, and 246 dogs.

▲ *Robert Peary in his Arctic outfit.*
Explorers bundled up in fur coats and
boots for expeditions to the polar regions.

Reaching the Pole

Peary sailed as far north as possible. Most of the crew then stayed behind while Peary and Matthew Henson used the sleds and dogs to push farther north. They believed they reached the Pole. Peary left a flag and a note in a tin in the ice, so those who came after him would know he had been there.

Peary had lost eight toes to frostbite on an earlier expedition. He later had the last two **amputated** because it was easier to walk with no toes than two toes!

◄ *Peary sailed north on the ship* Roosevelt, *captained by Robert Bartlett.*

amputated: cut off

Cook Versus Peary

When Peary returned home, he was **furious** to discover that Cook claimed to have reached the Pole first. He set out to prove that Cook was lying. He questioned Cook's two Inuit friends. He got powerful people to write to the newspapers. Soon people didn't know who to believe.

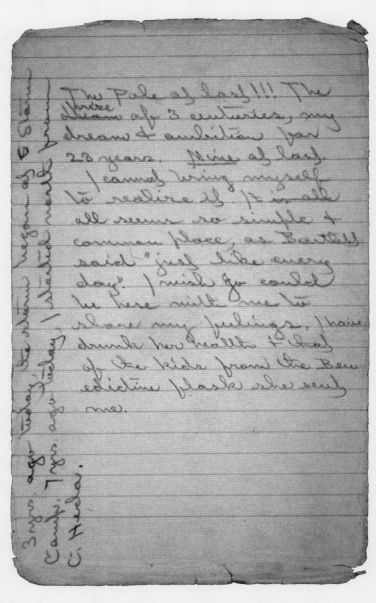

▲ *Peary wrote in his diary: "The pole at last!!! The prize of 3 centuries, my dream and ambition for 23 years. Mine at last."*

Who Got There First?

Who actually made it to the North Pole first? The public had problems with both their stories. Cook's records were missing. Peary had no instrument readings to prove how far north he had been. In the end, more people believed Peary than Cook.

◀ *The argument over who reached the North Pole first was world news. This is an illustration from a French newspaper of 1909.*

The first *confirmed* overland trip to the North Pole was not made until 1968. American adventurer, Ralph Plaisted, used a snowmobile to get there.

furious: very angry

The Canadian Expedition

Scientific Studies

After the North Pole had been **conquered**, expeditions wanted to explore and map the Arctic. The Canadian Arctic Expedition was a scientific exploration that set off in 1913. Canadian researchers hoped to map all the landmasses in the regions. They also wanted to identify the plants and animals that lived there.

▼ *The Canadian Arctic explorer Vilhjalmur Stefansson became so well-known that he was commemorated on a U.S. stamp.*

NORTH POLE

USA 22

Vilhjalmur Stefansson

A Bad Start

The expedition would use two groups to study different parts of the Arctic. Vilhjalmur Stefansson would lead the northern party. Rudolph Anderson would lead the southern one. The trip started badly. The weather was so bad in 1913 that the two ships were trapped in ice before they even reached the Arctic.

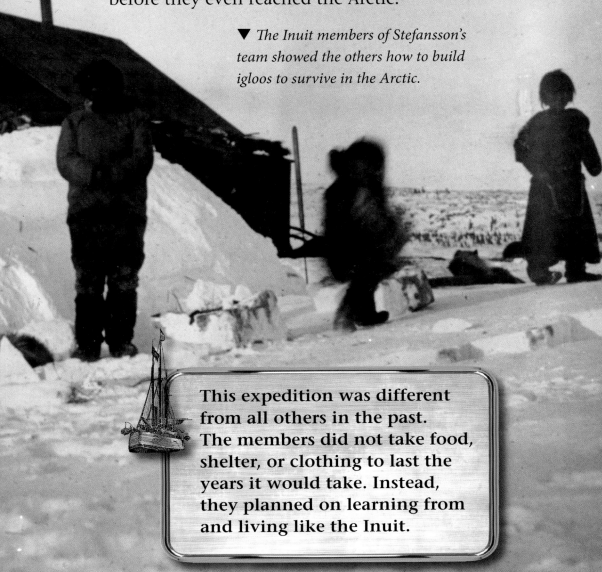

▼ *The Inuit members of Stefansson's team showed the others how to build igloos to survive in the Arctic.*

This expedition was different from all others in the past. The members did not take food, shelter, or clothing to last the years it would take. Instead, they planned on learning from and living like the Inuit.

conquered: successfully overcome

Crushed by the Ice

Stefansson and some of the crew left their ice-bound ship, the *Karluk*, to go off on a hunting trip. While they were gone, the ice shifted and carried the ship some distance away. The ice there pressed in and crushed the ship. The crew members who were still on board scrambled frantically onto the ice. The ship sank.

▼ *Captain Robert Bartlett (right) was an experienced Arctic explorer. He had been on Robert Peary's 1909 expedition to the North Pole.*

A Long Walk

The crew were **marooned** on drifting ice. They would not survive there without food or warm clothing, so two men, including Captain Bartlett, decided to walk over 700 miles (1,125 kilometers) to Wrangell Island in Russia for help. Amazingly, they made it. They came back with a ship and rescued the men that had survived.

Four crew members disagreed with Captain Bartlett's plan to walk to Wrangell Island for help. These men took sleds, dogs, and food and left on their own. They were never heard from again.

marooned: stranded, left without help

Mapping the Arctic

Stefansson was not put off by this failure. He found a new ship and crew, and set off again. He covered a huge part of the Arctic and discovered four new islands that even the Inuit did not know about. This meant they could correct older maps of the Arctic. They also proved that two areas—Croker Island and Keenan Land—did not exist at all!

▼ *Stefansson relied on the experience of the indigenous people. Here, they are building the dog-sleds used in the expedition.*

Collecting Specimens

The southern party returned with thousands of **specimens** of plants, animals, fossils, and rocks. They found important copper deposits and mapped the Mackenzie River Delta. Anderson's group also recorded the songs and culture of the Inuit for the first time.

The expeditions went to very remote regions. This meant there was no mail or news service. The Arctic explorers weren't even aware that World War I had begun!

▲ *The Mackenzie River is the longest river in Canada. The delta region, where it empties into the Arctic Ocean, was first mapped by Stefansson and his team.*

specimens: samples or examples of something

Amundsen's Expedition

Roald Amundsen was a Norwegian explorer. He was **inspired** by tales of John Franklin's doomed Arctic expedition. He thought that Franklin's ships were too large and that too many men had gone on the expedition. Amundsen wanted to be the first person to find the Northwest Passage.

▼ *After his journey to discover the Northwest Passage, Amundsen also became the first man to reach the South Pole, in 1911.*

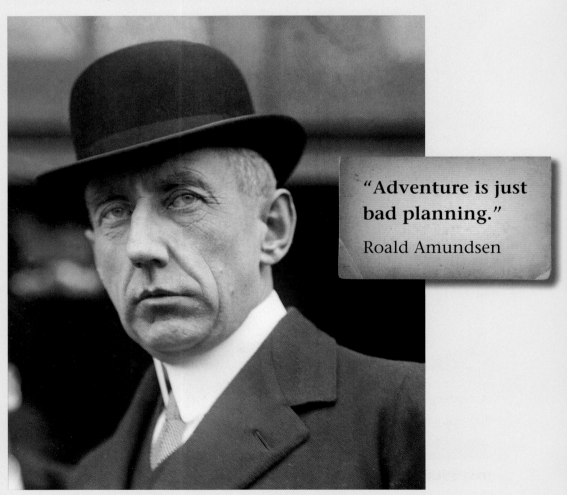

> "Adventure is just bad planning."
>
> Roald Amundsen

A New Way of Traveling

Amundsen set off in 1903. When he reached the edge of the Arctic, he used a small fishing boat. This could sail through much shallower waterways than the big ships used by other expeditions. Amundsen also took a crew of only six men. He planned to travel along the coast and live off the land.

▲ *During their expedition, Amundsen and his small crew relied on animals they caught for food rather than carrying many supplies with them.*

inspired: moved to action

A Two-Year Wait

Amundsen's ship, the *Gjoa*, made good progress at first. He and his crew anchored in a bay on King William Island, where Franklin's men had **perished**. But the *Gjoa* was then icebound for two years. The crew spent the time learning Inuit ways.

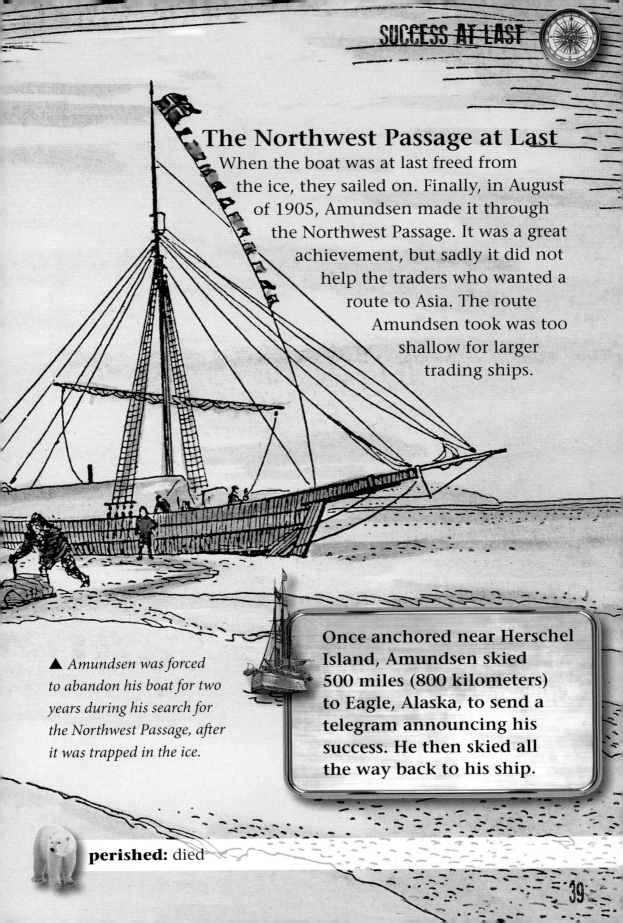

The Northwest Passage at Last

When the boat was at last freed from the ice, they sailed on. Finally, in August of 1905, Amundsen made it through the Northwest Passage. It was a great achievement, but sadly it did not help the traders who wanted a route to Asia. The route Amundsen took was too shallow for larger trading ships.

▲ *Amundsen was forced to abandon his boat for two years during his search for the Northwest Passage, after it was trapped in the ice.*

Once anchored near Herschel Island, Amundsen skied 500 miles (800 kilometers) to Eagle, Alaska, to send a telegram announcing his success. He then skied all the way back to his ship.

perished: died

The Arctic Today

What's Left to Discover?

There are still discoveries to make in the Arctic.
Historians want to know what happened to early
explorers who disappeared. The fate of Franklin's
expedition was a mystery for a long time. People
wondered why not even one person survived.

▼ *These headstones mark the site where the
bodies of Franklin's crew members were found
on Beechey Island, Nunavut.*

The Secrets of the Ice Mummies

In the 1980s, scientists found three bodies in the ice from Franklin's expedition. The freezing temperatures had preserved them like mummies. They examined them to find their cause of death. Tests showed that they had suffered from lead poisoning. Researchers wonder if lead poisoning played a part in the deaths of the rest of the crew.

Franklin's ships, the *Terror* and *Erebus*, have still not been found. Even so, they have already been named a National Historic Site by the Canadian government.

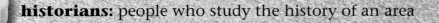

historians: people who study the history of an area

Problems with the Passage

There are still problems with the Northwest Passage. Different countries all claim that they own this important route. The Canadian government says that it belongs to Canada because it lies between the mainland and Canadian islands. Other countries think it should be an international waterway.

▼ *Governments are still trying to find a solution to the problem of ice closing the Northwest Passage for most of the year.*

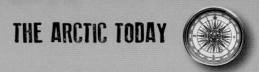

The Northwest Passage Today

So far only 11 international crossings have been made through the Passage since Amundsen's journey. Sea ice still blocks the way for most of the year. Climate change is when normal weather patterns in a particular place change over a long period of time. This is happening in the Arctic, and may mean that there will be open water for longer in the Northwest Passage.

"As Canadians, part of our core self-definition is that we are from the North. Proud of it. And the **epitomization** of what is the North is the Arctic."

Chris Hadfield, astronaut

epitomization: a perfect example of something

Climate Change

Climate change is affecting the Arctic in other ways, too. Melting sea ice means a loss of **habitat** and feeding grounds for many Arctic animals that hunt on the ice, such as polar bears.

▶ *Climate change is severely threatening the lifestyle and habitat of polar bears, and they are now a threatened species.*

▼ *Changes in the weather are also affecting the lives of the native Arctic peoples.*

The Inuit Under Threat

The culture and food supply of the Inuit is also at risk. They rely on the polar bears for food and clothing. The warmer weather means there is less ice, which makes it harder to build igloos. The Inuit also rely on hunting tourism to bring in money. But as the numbers of polar bears decline, so do the numbers of tourists.

Timeline

Pre-history Greeks (Pytheas) and Vikings travel to polar regions

1497 Russians sail around north coast of Norway looking for northeast route

1575 Martin Frobisher reaches Baffin Island

1606 John Knight dies while searching for Northwest Passage

1733 Great Northern Expedition to find route around north coast of Russia

1845 Sir John Franklin begins his doomed expedition

1850 Robert McClure sails to Arctic to find Franklin and his crew

1871 Charles Hall and the *Polaris* Expedition

1903 Roald Amundsen sails through the Northwest Passage

1907 North Pole attempt by Frederick Cook

1908 North Pole attempt by Robert Peary

1913 The Canadian Arctic Expedition with Stefansson and Anderson

habitat: the natural home of an animal

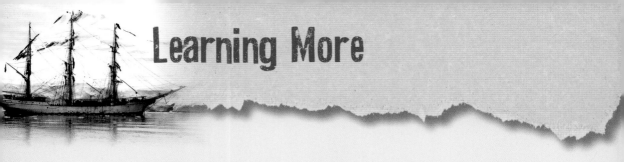

Learning More

Books

Sir John Franklin: The Search for the Northwest Passage
by Anders Knudesn
(Crabtree Publishing, 2007)

Henry Hudson: Seeking the Northwest Passage
by Carrie Gleason
(Crabtree Publishing, 2005)

Peary and Henson: The Race to the North Pole
by Baron Bedesky
(Crabtree Publishing, 2006)

Roald Amundsen
by Julie Karner
(Crabtree Publishing, 2007)

The Arctic
by Catherine Guigon
(Harry N. Abrams, 2007)

*Explorers Who Made It…
Or Died Trying*
by Frieda Wishinsky
(Scholastic Canada, 2011)

Websites

*http://www.spri.cam.ac.uk/
resources/kids/*
Polar exploration information from the Scott Polar Research Institute

*http://photography.
nationalgeographic.com/
photography/photos/north-
pole-expeditions/#/peary-arctic-
expedition_10496_600x450.jpg*
Photos from Robert Peary's expedition to the North Pole

*http://www.athropolis.com/links/
arctic.htm*
Arctic information for kids

*http://www.civilization.ca/
cmc/exhibitions/tresors/ethno/
etp0200e.shtml*
Photos and information about the Canadian Arctic Expedition

*http://www.enchantedlearning.
com/explorers/arctic.shtml*
Arctic explorers

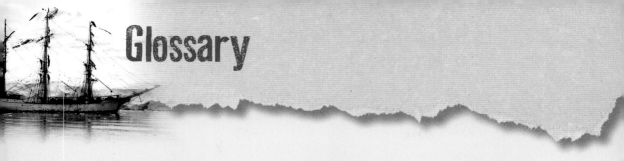

Glossary

adopted Used as their own

amputated Cut off

arsenic A gray, poisonous metal

conquered Successfully overcome

epitomization A perfect example of something

expeditions Journeys taken for a special purpose

furious Very angry

habitat The natural home of an animal

historians People who study the history of an area

hull The bottom and sides of a ship

hydrogen A gas that is lighter than air

ice floe A flat mass of ice floating on the sea

in earnest Make a serious attempt

indigenous Being born in or coming from a particular place

inspired Moved to action

marooned Stranded, left without help

perished Died

sabotaged Damaged on purpose

specimens Samples or examples of something

uninhabitable Not fit to live in

vanished Disappeared

Index

Entries in **bold** refer to pictures